What is a noun?

Ans. Any Name of the person Place Animal or Thing or an Idea is a noun.

What is a proper noun?

Ans. Name of the person or place is a proper noun.

What is a common noun?

Ans. Name of an animal or Thing is a common noun.

*Identify the name of the person or place (proper noun) in the following sentence.

Sameer went to Goa last night.

 *Identify the animal and thing (common noun) in the following sentence.

Loin is the King of the jungle.

Mother bought bananas.

What type of noun is ' jungle'?

Jungle is a place but it is not a proper noun.

As when we say jungle it can mean any jungle of the world.

What is a collective noun?

When a group of things is referred using one word we say that it is a collective noun.

For example-Father, Mother, Son and Daughter can be together referred as a 'Family'.

Identify the collective noun in the following sentences

Our team won the match.

Here team is the collective noun as team refers to a group of people.

What is an abstract noun?

'Feelings 'refers to an abstract noun.

For example-Sam is feeling hungry

Here 'hungry' refers to an abstract noun as we can feel hunger but cannot touch or see it.

What is a concrete noun?

Anything we can feel or touch is a concrete noun.

For example-Will you please pass that ball?

Here ball is a concrete noun as we can touch and play with the ball.

What is a countable noun?

Those things which we can count using number or measurements are countable noun.

For example-Father bought juicy mangoes.

Here mangoes are countable noun as we can count the mangoes.

What is an uncountable noun?

Those things which we cannot count or are extremely difficult to count are uncountable noun.

For example-Please give me some water.

Here some can be any quality of water for example a glass, a bucket etc.

*What is an Idea?

Idea refers to a quality.

For Example-Mother speaks politely.

Here 'politely' refers to a quality.

India got the freedom.

Here 'freedom' is the quality of the country India.

NAME: ______________________   DATE: __________

Noun Search

Directions: Read the sentences below. Circle the nouns.

1. The kids went to the mountains.
2. They stayed at a big cabin.
3. The cabin had lots of games.
4. The boys built a fort using snow.
5. The girls built a snowman.
6. They decorated it with a scarf and hat.
7. That night, their parents built a fire.
8. The kids toasted marshmallows.
9. Then, the family watched a movie.
10. They ate popcorn and candy.
11. Later, they read a book.
12. The trip was so much fun!

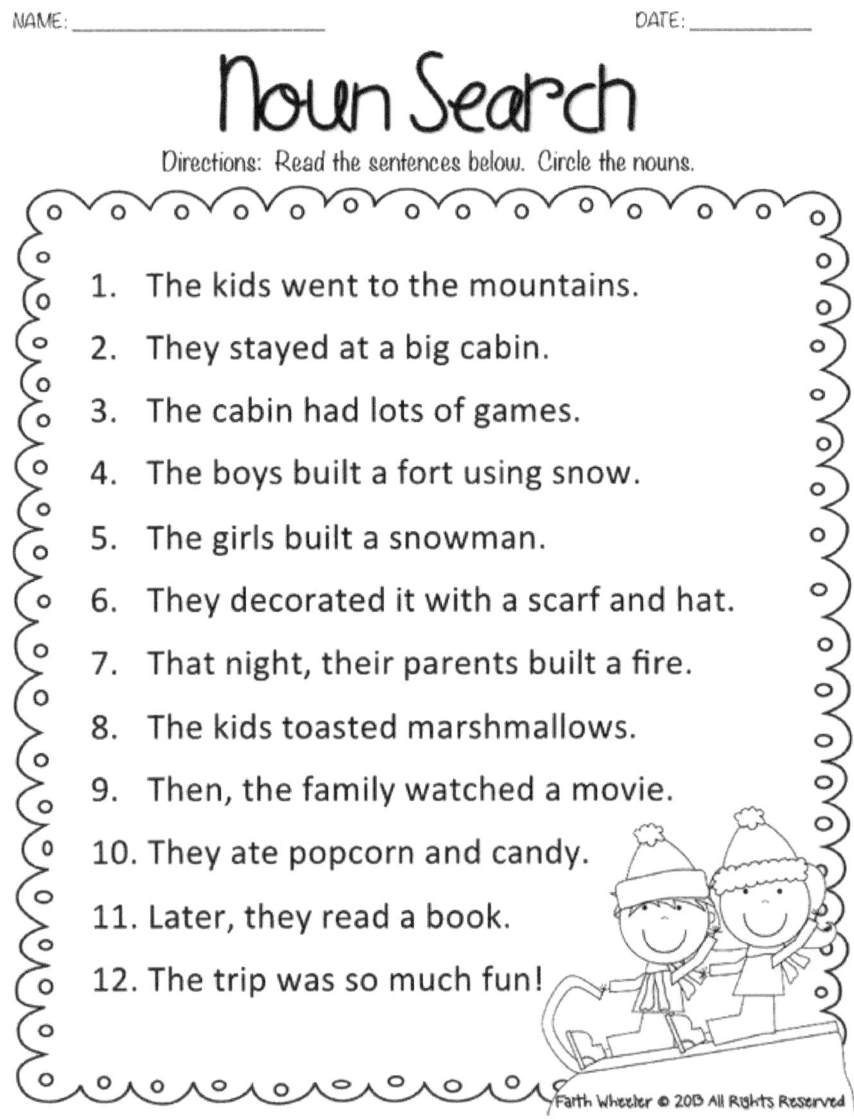

What is a verb?

> **Verbs** are words that express an action or a state of being. The main verb of a sentence is usually found at the beginning and followed by the subject, while auxiliary verbs are used to complete various tenses.
> **For example:**
> • He went home early after he was done with work.

Anything that indicates movement or action is a verb

For example-Seema is talking Here talking indicates the movement of the mouth hence 'talking' is a verb.

Find the Verbs!

A verb is a word that describes an action or a state of being. Can you find all the verbs in the following sentences? Circle the verbs you discover!

1. It was very cold yesterday.

2. The kids are very loud.

3. Sheena is sick today.

4. Mom got a new pair of shoes.

5. Ted is watching a movie.

6. The sun rises from the east.

7. Mr. Larson talked on the phone.

8. She ran across the bridge.

9. Marnie lives in the blue house.

Name: _______________________
Date : _______________________

Doing Words

Complete these sentences using the doing words in the box. Then read them aloud.

fly	play	sit	feeds	swims

1. Birds ____________.
2. The duck ____________.
3. Rohan ____________ the duck.
4. Yashu and Charu ____________ on the seesaw.
5. Father and mother ____________ on the bench.

Complete these sentences with the correct form of the doing words in the boxes. Then read them aloud.

1. a. Do you ____________ to music?
    b. Rishi ____________ to songs on the television.   listen

2. a. Mishu and Tashu ____________ letters every week.
    b. Aaina ____________ a letter to her friend.   write

3. a. Ruby ____________ to the park.
    b. I ____________ to school.   walk

4. a. Grandma ____________ coconut water.
    b. I ____________ a lot of water every day.   drink

5. a. I ____________ with my friends.
    b. Ritul ____________ badminton with Anshika every evening.   play

What is an adjective?

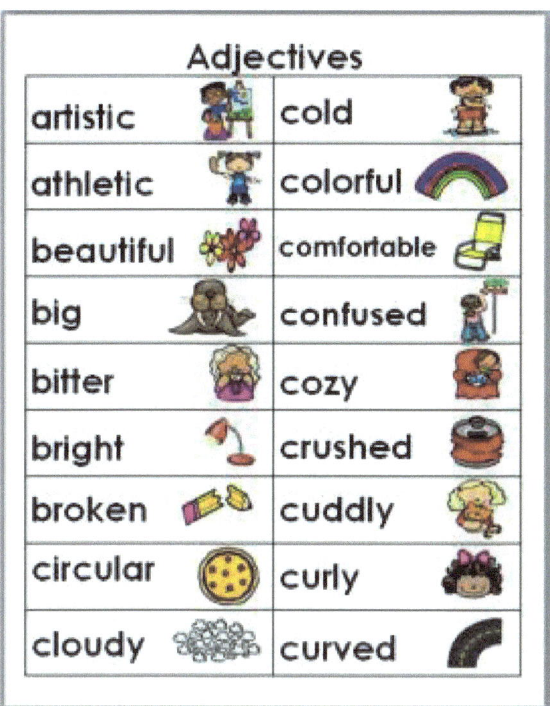

The word which tells us more about the noun is an adjective.

Adjective is used to describe size, shape, colour, taste quality or quantity.

For example-The shirt is blue in colour.

Here blue is an adjective as it tells us something more about the shirt.

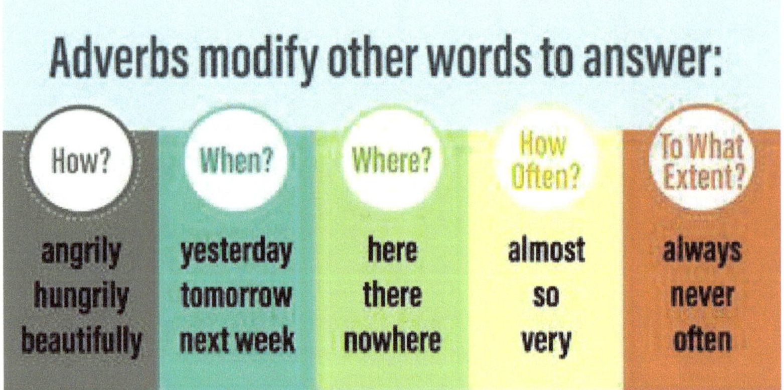

What is an adverb?

Adverb tells us how the work is being performed

For Example-The boy writes very slowly.

Here slowly tells us how the boy writes, hence slowly is an adverb.

What is a Pronoun?

A Pronoun is used instead of a noun. It is a short form of a noun.

For example-The cat is black in colour. The cat is hungry.

Instead of speaking the word 'The cat' again and again. We can use the pronoun 'it'

And frame the sentence as -The cat is black in colour. It is very hungry

Note-We cannot start a sentence with the pronoun itself as people will not understand whom we are talking about

*For male we use the pronoun 'He'

*For female we use the pronoun 'She'

*For animals and things, we use the Pronoun 'it

*For more than one person we use "they /them'

*When people are talking in a group or taking a group decision then 'We' is used.

What is a preposition?

Preposition tells us where a particular name, place, animal or a thing is.

For example- Mother sits on the ground here on is a preposition.

*A preposition is mostly located after a verb

1) The clock is ....the wall.

2) The ball is ....the table.

3) The cat is ....the armchair.

4) The table is ....the armchair.

5) The carpet is ....the floor.

6) The lamp is ....the table.

7) The flowers are ....the vase.

8) The table is ....the chair and the armchair.

What is a conjunction?

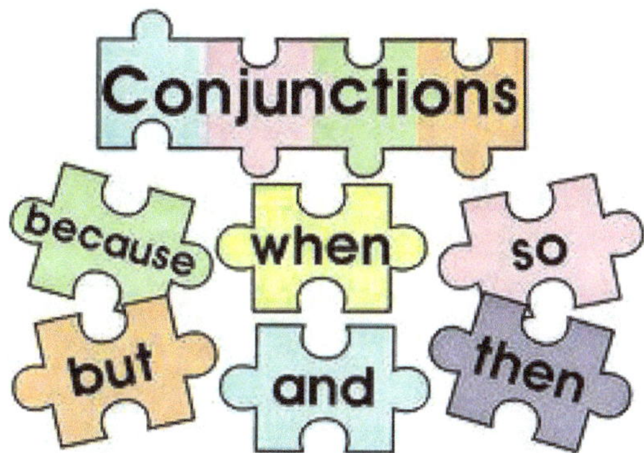

A conjunction is used to join two sentences having similar or different piece of information.

For example-I like ice-creams. I like chocolates.

These two sentences can be written as I like chocolates and ice-creams.

I like to play.

I don't like to study.

This can be combined as -I like to play but I don't like to study.

Give me a pen. Give me a pencil.

This can be combined as-Give me a pen and a pencil

I was late. It was raining.

This can be combined as-

I was late because it was raining.

I was late as it was raining.

It was raining so I was late.

Coordinating Conjunctions Worksheet

and	but	so	or	for

Complete the sentence with correct conjunction:

1. Ron laughed cheerfully ______ jumped out.

2. She is poor ______ she is kind.

3. Emma asked me a doubt, ______ I replied.

4. Tina ______ Tim are best friends.

5. I was tired, ______ I went to home early.

6. She refused at first, ______ finally accepted it.

7. I buy cakes, candies ______ ice-creams.

8. I have got an exam tomorrow, ___ I must study tonight.

9. Do you prefer coffee ______ tea?

10. I have waited at the airport ______ three hours.

What is a tense?

Tense Chart With Rules And Examples

Zehernews.com	Present	Past	Future
Simple	I write a letter. S+V1+O	I wrote a letter. S+was/were+V1+ing+O	I shall write a letter. S+shall/will+V1+O
Continuous	I am writing a letter. S+is/am/are+V1+ing+O	I was writing a letter. S+was/were+V1+ing+O	I shall be writing a letter. S+shall/will+be+V1+ing+O
Perfect	I have written a letter. S+have/has+V3+O	I had written a letter. S+had+V3+O	I shall have written a letter. S+shall/will+have+been+V3+O
Perfect Continuous	I have been writing a letter. S+have/has+been+V1+ing+O	I had been writing a letter. S+had+been+V1++ing+O	I shall have been writing a letter. S+shall/will+have+been+V1+ing+O

S=Subject   O=Object   V=Verb

Tense tells us about the 'time"

Which time the tense tells us about?

The tense tells us about that time when a particular work in performed.

What is a present tense?

If the work is performed 'right now' it is present tense.

For example-I read about tense (रीड)

What is a past tense?

If the work is performed just before a minute it is past tense.

For example-I opened the mobile.

What is a future tense?

If the work is yet to be performed it is future tense

For example-I will keep the mobile aside.

SR #	SENTENCES	ANSWER
01.	Jack had been working in this office for five years.	Past Perfect Continuous Tense
02.	They walk daily.	
03.	Tom will leave for Canada tomorrow.	
04.	She is working hard to pass the exam.	
05.	Why were you smoking?	
06.	He has been playing the chess since evening.	
07.	Tom will have read the novel by the end of this month.	
08.	I am enjoying the holidays.	
09.	He will be watching the movie at 9 pm.	
10.	He has been painting the door for an hour.	
11.	I had finished my work before you arrived.	
12.	He was reading the novel yesterday.	
13.	Jack will attend the meeting on Tuesday.	
14.	They had been living in this town since 2008.	
15.	He has successfully completed his graduation.	
16.	Joe will have got admission in college by December.	
17.	Jackson reads newspaper in the morning.	
18.	Sara will have been attending ESL Classes for two months.	
19.	I have been learning Spanish for one week.	
20.	The patient took medicine.	
21.	Jim had finished the meal before the door bell rang.	
22.	Joe has won the best employee award of the year.	
23.	Tim will have been visiting Europe for two weeks.	
24.	The kids were playing in the park.	
25.	They are going to Austria to spend holidays.	

What is an article?

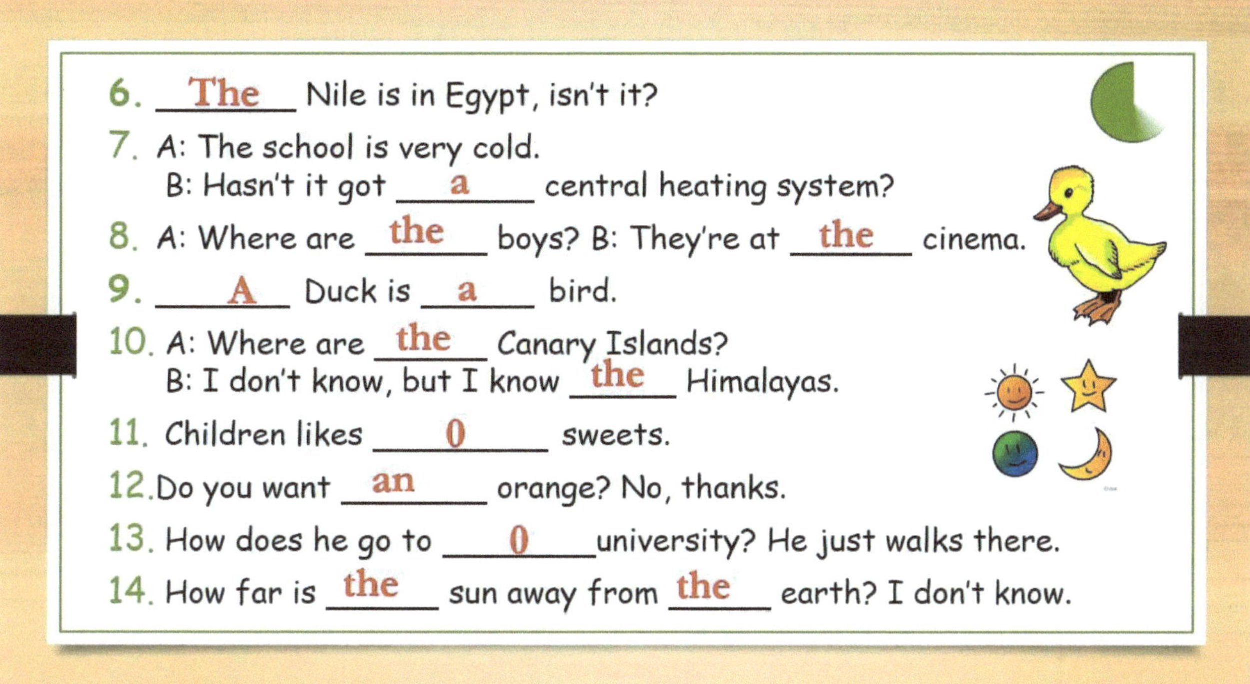

An article is usually put before a common noun

A, An and The are the articles

'A' is generally put before a common noun

For example-a boy, a baby

'An' is generally put before a vowel

For example-An apple, An elephant, An ice cube, An orange, An Umbrella

The is generally used for Plurals or if any additional information is given about a subject.

For example-A man (Singular) The man (Plural)

The shirt is Blue in colour

*Here shirt is a common noun but since additional information is given about the shirt (Blue in colour) We start with 'The'

The is also used before things the are unique and only one in nature

For Example-The Sun, The Moon, The stars, The sky etc.

Name:	Class:	Date:

Articles: (a, an, the)

Complete the passage with the (a, an, the) then complete the tasks:

It was _______ weekend, Larry got out of bed at nine thirty. He went to ________ bathroom, had a wash and got dressed. He went downstairs, made coffee and pancakes for everyone and took it into ______ living room and put them on ______ coffee table next to ____ TV. He does this twice ____ week, as ____ treat for his wife Lara. During ____ week she always gets up early to get ____ kids ready for school. She takes them to school and then she goes to university. She is ____ student and she is attending ____ art course there. At the moment, their children are still in bed. They went to bed quiet late last night. Later they are going to ____ beach for ______ day. Larry turned on ____ TV to watch ______ episode of Emmerdale. Then he went back to ____ bedroom and opened ________ curtains. Lara was already awake as she could smell ______ pancakes and coffee. Larry is ____ good help around ______ house. He makes everyone breakfast, takes them out and is ____ excellent dad too. They will be leaving ______ house in ____ hour or two to Scarborough. All the children came running into ______ bedroom and sat on ______ bed, all excited about going to ______ beach.

Answer the following in full sentences:

1. Who woke up at nine thirty? ____
2. What did he make? ____
3. Where was his wife? ____
4. Where are they going for the day? ____
5. Where did the children sit before breakfast? ____

Circle (True) or (False). And then correct all mistakes:

1. This story happened on a weekday.   True   False
2. Larry didn't put the TV on.   True   False
3. Larry is a good family man.   True   False
4. Lara is a university lecturer.   True   False
5. They are going to the beach next week.   True   False

Discussion: What is your father like? Is he a good family man?

This book is available on Amazon and Flipkart

This book is available on Amazon and Flipkart